I0790454

UNNATURAL BEHAVIOR
WHERE ARE WE GOING?

Michael Walker

INTRODUCTION

The year is 2055, and it's a standing floor in the Senate. Lawmakers are going back and forth trying to resolve the issue of serial killers in the thousands that are killing women and children to having sexual relations with their corpses. The debate is over a bill that's up for a vote, let's call it proposal 25a, which legalizes necrophilia.

This Bill passed the Congress by a majority vote a few weeks earlier. Some of those in favor of the new law, want to legalize necrophilia to stop the killing of innocent women and children by the necrophiliacs, for the purpose of sexual gratification.

Just outside of the White House and Capitol Hill, there are hundreds of necrophiliac demonstrators, and their supporters with picket signs, waving the American flag, along with their spokesperson who we will call, Mr. Ridgeway, a third-generation decedent of one of the most famous necrophiliac serial killers, Gary Ridgeway (The Green River Killer).

They are determined and serious about their fight. We can hear them in the media saying things like "we are not hurting anyone; we just want our rights". They are speaking to people like CNN Anchor Anderson Cooper III, ABC News correspondent Bob Woodruff III, and

MSNBC news correspondent Ed Shultz III like and others.

This debate has been going on for the past few years, and it was something that needed to be addressed due to the increase in necrophiliac activity.

The spike in these types of crimes came as a direct result of another bill that finally passed about 10 years earlier. Let's call it Proposal 18b, which legalizes zoophilia (those who have sex or sexual relationships with animals). Similar protest proceeded and took place when they too were on capitol hill fighting for their rights to have sexual relationships or even marry animals.

So as the week passed, and after going back and forth in Congress, just like similar bills that proceeded it, it passed the Senate unanimously, as it also passed thru Congress a few weeks earlier.

Now only one thing left, and that's for the President of the United States to sign off on it, which he or she agreed to do if the law passed Congress. Done!!!! The following morning. So, now necrophilia is legal and a victory is in place for this sick and twisted people, and others who supported it.

The President's take on this was one that sounds all too familiar, he or she made comments like, well; I don't do it, and my kids or family members don't do it, but they are not hurting anyone, and if it would save lives, then we need to pass this. Besides, it's the right thing to do as the number of those practicing this type of behavior in reaching the millions.

Strange huh? Sick Huh? Unbelievable Huh? Twisted Huh? And I bet those of you who are reading this will also say unlikely, huh? We will never go this far, huh?

Well, what if I told you that your grand-parents and possibly your parents over 30 years ago never thought we would see same sex marriages legalized. What if I also told you that when the idea of same sex marriages came up, your grand-parents and possibly your parents used the same phrases to describe same sex marriages, phrases like strange, twisted, sick and unlikely. But here we are, over 30 plus years later and more and more states are legalizing same sex marriages and it's only a matter of time before all 52 states legalize it.

So where are we going with this or better yet, where am I going with this? How far is too far? When will we, or it stop, how liberal are we going to become in future years? I'll answer that in a later segment of the book, but let's look at how this whole thing started.

INTERRACIAL MARRAIGES

In 1967, interracial marriages finally became legal in almost all 50 states after a long-drawn-out fight on the Capitol. So how did they get there?

We'll, it started long before the civil rights movement and even slavery. But before I get into details on this, let's look at the perception of those who lived before it became legal, and what they were probably thinking back then.

After the civil war, the general consensus was that everybody stuck with their own kind, and that mixing race was unacceptable and unnatural behavior. Those who participated in interracial relationships were mostly doing it in secrecy. The majority of those living in that time frowned upon those who would part-take in such activities, particularly whites in this country, who thought they were the dominant species and didn't deem people of color as human beings. They too perhaps also used some of the same phrases that I used earlier in describing necrophilia, to describe interracial marriages, like strange, twisted, sick and unlikely.

Those who would dare get caught participating in such behavior, would be subject to assaults, imprisonment, and in some cases death. Even if you didn't have a problem who others dating outside the race but it wasn't your thing, back then, you would have certainly not voiced your opinion, and definitely not taken a stand.

You see, to those that lived before and especially after the civil war (whites and blacks) particularly in the south, this would be something that would never become legal, and that we as a country will never allow any law to pass approving such behavior. Before the Civil War, it was not a common practice but after the Civil War, since slaves were freed, people were starting to date or at least attempt to date and have open relationships and sexual relationships with those outside their race. Of course, now, we see interracial couples in most areas and we don't even give it a second look, because it's the new normal. So here we are in 2015 and its legal, alive, and working without resistance. It's very common and acceptable.

Now by no means am I saying that this is wrong, sick, and twisted because we are all living human beings, and we are of opposite sex as the source intended it to be, just different pigmentation. I'm simply using it as a starting point of what we don't accept early on, to what we grow to accept over time. So here are some following details.

In the year 1664, "Maryland passed a law banning white women from marrying black men". This was well before the USA became a nation and well before the Revolutionary War. Then in 1691, "The Commonwealth of Virginia bans all interracial marriages", this was the actual start of this perception. We then fast forward to 1780, where the first steps to abolish slavery was set in place by the state of Pennsylvania who repeals the law passed in

1691; It failed. Things pretty much remained the same for almost another 50 plus years. Now before we move forward, let's review how people saw mixing races back then.

It was very uncommon for whites and blacks in this country to marry or even attempt to get married outside of their race.

Blacks were mainly slaves, and even whites who were in control, did not have the right to marry their slaves or any blacks for that matter.

If we really examine how things really were back then, we might even say that the number of those who were interested in marrying outside the race were few and far between. The number of those interested in such behavior was very low. I can't tell you how low those numbers were, but if you can imagine the perception of those for instance that are interested in say zoophile (having sexual relations or relationships with animals) is right now in 2020, then I would think those numbers are similar.

You can see here the correlation between what was common place verses what was deemed unacceptable, unlikely, sick, twisted, and strange. You see those living in those times frowned heavily on interracial marriages. In fact, I bet if you were to sit down with the average white person to support this and speak about it, not even from the south back then, they would have used these same phrases, and probably have thrown you out of their house. I even believe if you would have spoken to some slaves back then, they might have had the same perception, and maybe even thrown you out of their slave quarters. You see it was uncommon, and unnatural behavior to do such things back then and there were only small pockets of people participating in such activities, well, at least in the open.

Now by no means am I one that's against interracial marriages, because I understand that this is a union between a male and female of the human race, just different pigmentation, but by the standards of the 1700's, I too, would have not condoned such behavior because I too just like everyone else back then, probably would have deemed it unnatural due too it being something our ancestors were against, and it was not commonplace back then.

Now we fast forward to 1843 where it becomes a little bit more common, and now the fight to repeal the previous laws on banning interracial marriages begins. That year, Massachusetts, makes a second stand to repeal the law; It fails. Then in 1883, after the Civil War, the case of Pace vs Alabama goes to the Supreme Court and they rule unanimously, that state level bans Tony Pace and Mary Cox from marriage, an interracial couple. They were both arrested under section 4189, they were sentenced to seven years each. Then fast forward a few years to 1912, Rep. Seaborn Roddenberg a Georgia Democrat makes a second attempt to revise the constitution to ban interracial marriages in all 50 states.

Following that in 1922, Congress passes Cable Act, stripping the citizenship of any U.S. citizen who married "an alien ineligible for citizenship", this was designed to target Asian Americans at the time. Now although when I speak about interracial marriages, we often think about black and white couples, but there were also others in this country back then that frowned upon other race mixing as well. So, as we see from the 1922 law, this was un-natural behavior for other ethnic backgrounds also.

We move on to 1928, where Senator Coleman Blease, a democrat from South Carolina, who was also a proud member of the Klu Klux Klan and former Governor of that state, makes another attempt to revise the constitution to ban interracial marriages. It failed.

Now, let's take a look at where we were at that point. Interracial marriages in the 1920'S were becoming more and more common, and even though some didn't have a problem with it even in the 1800's, it was starting to become widely accepted, and more and more people were coming out in support of it, mainly because more and more people were doing it, or knew someone who was.

You see, it went from widely unacceptable, to commonplace over a period of time, what most deemed as unnatural behavior was becoming more natural, and if you were to ask people living in the 1600's to late 1800's, they would have never expected it to go that far, meaning getting to the point where hundreds or thousands of people were doing it to the point where we have to take the fight to the Capitol.

Back in the 1600's to the mid 1800's, there were probably only small pockets of people participating in this type of activity, and there was not a real strong need to object to it because those people were considered sick, and twisted, and nobody perhaps wanted to be around them, so they arrested them. Can you see where I'm going with this?

So, we fast forward to the 1967 movie Guess Who's Coming to Dinner, which was produced and directed by Stanley Kramer, and written by William Rose featuring the great actors Sidney Poitier, and Katharine Hepburn. At that point, we are now geared toward a showdown to allow interracial marriages to become legal in every state because now it has hit the mainstream media in film.

The movie depicts a family doctor who is African American, falling for and getting engaged to one of his patient's daughters (a white female). Both of their parent's dads strongly oppose the marriage based on values instilled in them from their previous generation. Eventually both dads decide to let down guards and support the marriage primarily because the times call for them to do so.

This is the thing about change that some reading this won't see. You see, time determines what becomes acceptable based on the number of people doing a particular thing, and then when everyone, or the majority of people start doing something, even if it's against our morals, or the way we were taught, then we just accept it.

One may also refer to the big kiss between Captain Kirk and Uhora on Star Trek around the same time frame, which stirred up even more controversy because that was actually on TV and not a movie. This caused outrage among most whites in this country because even thou this was going on, seeing it on a TV show that had so much influence over popular culture at the time just confirmed it was happening.

You see, once a particular behavior is brought to the big screen, or even television, we allow our kids, and ourselves to take it into consideration and start to mellow down, and accept something as natural behavior, that was once not in our character to do so.

In the case of Loving vs Virginia in 1967, ironically the same year the movie came out, the Supreme Court ruled in favor of Loving overturning Pace vs Alabama, stating the state law violates the Fourteenth Amendment to the US Constitution.

Chief Justice Earl Warren wrote:

"There is patently no legitimate overriding purpose independent of invidious racial discrimination which justifies this classification. The fact that Virginia prohibits only interracial marriages involving white persons demonstrates that the racial classifications must stand on their own justification, as measures designed to maintain White Supremacy ...

"The freedom to marry has long been recognized as one of the vital personal rights essential to the orderly pursuit of happiness by free men ... To deny this fundamental freedom on so unsupportable a basis as the racial classifications embodied in these statutes, classifications so directly subversive of the principle of equality at the heart of the <u>Fourteenth Amendment</u>, is surely to deprive all the State's citizens of liberty without due process of law. The Fourteenth Amendment requires that the freedom of choice to marry not be restricted by invidious racial discriminations. Under our Constitution, the freedom to marry, or not marry, a person of another race resides with the individual and cannot be infringed by the State."

From that point on interracial marriages became legal in all 50 states. Well, except for Alabama, which made it legal in the year 2000.

So now where are we? Well, we are in a comfortable commonplace for interracial marriages. We all see interracial couples everywhere we go and most of us don't even think twice about it but if it were say, 70 plus years ago, all parties involved would have definitely turned heads and possibly been arrested, assaulted, and in some cases murdered. I myself have even dated outside the race and could not imagine not having the right to do so. But if my great, great grandparents were still alive, the family possibly might have dis-owned me, cut me out, and also shared their concerns to me that this type of behavior would be unacceptable, twisted, un-natural behavior to them. I'm sure it would probably even be the same for you no matter what background you came from. Yea, we still have those who frown on it, but those numbers are now few and far between, unlike back in the day when the majority of those dating outside the race were far and between. It's reverse now.

In the late 1960's, it was really starting to hit the fan. The hippie movement preached free love, and there was a lot of interracial mixing taking place. I'm sure they were even in the media saying things like we are not hurting anyone; we just want our rights.

You see, we now accept something as commonplace that we never envisioned accepting as commonplace 60 plus years ago. And it's as normal as a regular marriage. So, what's next? Where are we going? Who's on deck or stepping up to the plate? Well, how about we look at where are we now. Follow me! Well, have you been reading the papers and watching the news? I have, and I see a trend, I see something coming into play that I could have not ever dreamed of as a youth, but here we are. You follow me yet? Where are we now? Same Sex Marriages.

SAME SEX MARRAIGES:

Now this is where things begin to get a little tricky, so before I begin here, let me start by saying that I'm not bashing gays or lesbians, in fact, I know plenty of them, and have worked with many of them in past years, and by nature, they are some of the nicest, coolest, and kindest people you ever wanna meet. But if you are a Bible or Islam believer, then you would say that being of the same sex and marrying is un-natural behavior, but also let me state that if you are a religious believer and reading this, then you know not to judge anyone either as God is all of our judge, you can only pray for them, love them, and let God determine what is acceptable to him.

Again, let me re-iterate, I'm not speaking badly of gays or lesbians, nor am I comparing them to what's to come in later chapters, I'm simply making a symbolic point, so please don't get offended if you are reading this book, and you are gay or lesbian, it's just a correlation from something that was not unacceptable, to what could become acceptable at a later date; But, by no means are you in that category on what's to come, and neither are those in the interracial marriage section for that matter. But I do have grounds for writing this book and I'm sorry to say, that your fight will be the pivotal fight for what could eventually happen in this country and around the rest of the world. I can't judge any of you as I have my own problems and may have to get right with my maker, myself. So don't let my opinion or writing cause a rift between myself and your fight. And in saying that, let me continue.

So let me begin this segment by saying, about 30 plus years ago, if you would tell anyone living back then, including myself that same sex marriages would be legal in some states, you would have probably thought that that's crazy, and used some of the same terms like, not possible, unacceptable, unbelievable, strange, and twisted, but look around, here we are on the verge of getting same sex marriages legal in every state. Give it a few years, this is where we are now. So how did it start? Well let's take a look.

Gays and Lesbians have been fighting for their rights for hundreds of years now, but just like interracial marriages, they were in the closest and were few in numbers, or at least as far as we knew. The fight really started to gain momentum as states progressed into legalizing interracial marriages. Once interracial marriages came into full circle, then the next fight began.

In the late 1960's, more and more gays and lesbians were coming out protesting and demanding to have the same rights as heterosexual couples. Prior to the late 1960's, they were scrutinized, ridiculed, assaulted, imprisoned, and in some countries put to death for this behavior, because just like interracial marriages, this was considered unnatural behavior. Most were ashamed to even let people know they were gay or lesbian. It wasn't just deemed unnatural behavior to Christians, but even to other sects, colonies, races, and religions, including Muslims.

The major beginning in the U.S. was the Stonewall riots in 1969, this was a pure gay rights movement that unified gays and lesbians and prompted the next fight shortly after we just got through the interracial marriage issue.

Also, in England, Canada and a few other countries, around the same time, they began to decriminalize homosexual behavior. We fast forward a little further into the early 1970's, to see that gays and lesbians came out of the closest like never before.

They even began to enter politics.

In 1977, Harvey Milk became the first openly gay man to be elected to public office. He won a seat on the San Francisco Board of Supervisors. Eleven months later, he was assassinated. So just like most fights in this country, we have a martyr.

Someone who gets assassinated to further the fight. Now, in this fight, I'm sure there were more and possibly will be more to come.

The protest began to become more and more intense, and the number of those practicing in such behavior grew rapidly. By the end of the 1980's, those who were gay or lesbian, were not ashamed to be seen, or have family members, friends, and even the world know that they were gay or lesbian. I'm sure they were making comments in the media like "we are not hurting anyone; we just want our rights".

You see, if you look at the plight of this so far, just as the interracial couples were ashamed and embarrassed to let people know what they were up too, the exact same thing took place with gays and lesbians.

Now we fast forward to the early 1990's, the case of Baehr verse Lewin. In 1993, "the judge ruled that states have to give a concrete and compelling reason why gays should not have the same legal right to marry as heterosexual couples".

The previous case of Baehr verse Lewin actually influenced The Defense of Marriage Act a few years later. This was a law designed to counter same sex marriages and stop or slow down the fight. This was also a law that those who deemed same sex marriages as un-natural behavior a strong stand.

The Defense of Marriage Act states that "for the purpose of Federal Law, marriage was only possible for one man and one woman".

The Act actually stalled the fight for same sex marriages but it came up a few years later in the late 1990's.

In 1999, Civil Unions were formed. The purpose of these Civil Unions was to give same sex couples the same equal rights as heterosexual couples.

Fast forward to 2003, a Massachusetts Supreme court judge ruled "that gays had the same rights to marriage as heterosexual couples". Then, in May of 2004, Massachusetts became the 1st state in the Union to approve same sex marriages. Connecticut soon followed and in 2008, California got on board which made a huge impact.

The other determining factor to look at is mainstream media. Yes, mainstream media. If you recall in the previous chapter, we spoke about a movie "Guess Who's Coming to Dinner" and a scene from a TV series, "Star Trek", those two events without a doubt, helped the fight to legalize same interracial marriages in the late 1960's. So where are we now media wise? Well, let's take a look.

To the best of my knowledge or at least as far as I can remember, gays and lesbians have been referenced in film quite often over the past 20 plus years. The 1st reference of film that comes to my mind was the crying game back in 1992 starting Stephen Rea, Jaye Davison, Miranda Richardson and Forest Whitaker. This was the first time I ever remember hearing about this this type of activity on the big screen, I'm sure there were others back then, but I wasn't looking for them, and due to my heterosexual lifestyle and Christian up-bringing, of course, I had no interest.

We fast forward to another blockbuster smash, Brokeback Mountain, which was released in 2006, starting Heath Ledger, Jack Gyllenhaai, Anne Hathaway, Michelle Williams and Randy Quaid.

These are the only two that comes to mind, now if you look at the actors involved in those projects, there are some big names in there, condoning the same sex marriage fight, just like the fight before it (interracial marriages). I'm quite sure this would give them some strong credibility and ammo, as big time Hollywood actors support their movement.

The next thing we will look at is the impact in network television as we did with interracial marriages. When we think about how the media embrace gays and lesbians on TV, we can see a stronghold on popular culture. To the best of my knowledge, I remember Will and Grace as the first time I witnessed this on TV. Again, I'm not stating a fact here as I am sure there were others, but this is the 1st one that I remember off hand or at least what first comes to mind.

We fast forward to 2015, now, if we look at the trend, we start to come up with all kinds of examples of this. There is a large variety to choose from with at least one gay or lesbian character. You have Modern Family, Madam Secretary, Gotham, and Empire, just to name a few. Pretty mainstream huh? Well, there's more. They even have their own gay and lesbian networks and channels like The Logo Channel.

So based just on the media fact along, what makes you think that same sex marriages won't be legalized soon in every state.

Now at present 2020, there are at least 27 states that have passed laws or acts to ban gay marriages, but at least 10, count em, 10 current states have given same sex couples the same equal rights as heterosexual couples.

So, by this you are probably thinking, it would never happen, because 10 is a small number compared to 52, and some others of you may be even thinking if it did happen, we are light years away from that huh? Well, what if I told you, we may be a lot closer than you think. You see, just like the interracial movement, it only took a few instances, situations, and states to get the ball rolling, and others, due to the massive number of people supporting the movement in their home states, people like Governors, Mayors, Congressman, and Senators, are gonna have to get on board soon if they want to keep their jobs, and keep their approval ratings high.

Here is the thing, over 30 plus years ago, a Senator, Governor, Congressman, Mayor, or even a President didn't have to worry about pleasing gays and lesbians because the number of supporters were just too small. Also, the number of active gays and lesbians (out of the closest) were far and between. But if you look around now, you cannot sit here and read this, and think that you don't know at least a handful of gay or lesbian people, Also, you may even be of some kind of religious faith that tells you that this is unnatural behavior, but due to the fact that you know some of these people, or have some kind of a connection to them, you have sympathy. Your natural response would be to support them especially if you have a family member that's in this fight, even if it's something that you don't condone.

Strange huh? Sick Huh? Unbelievable Huh? Twisted Huh? Well, here we go again with those terms. You see when you get to the point of accepting something that years ago, you could never envision accepting, and you see more and more masses of people doing it, you brain meter that used those phrases in the past like strange, twisted, sick, and unbelievable starts to mild down. Once this happens, you start to reason with yourself and think things like, well they aren't hurting anyone, so I guess it's cool, I won't ever do it, that's unnatural, but it seems that thousands upon thousands of people are doing it now, so it can't be all that bad. This is what leads to acceptance, this is what makes us more liberal, when we clearly had a strong stance against certain things in the pasts. Ironically, when it comes to this issue (the issue of same sex marriages) we as average Americans don't even have the biggest problem. Christian preachers do.

Well, what if you are a Christian Minster? Then what? Will you let them in your church? Will you marry them? If they are in large numbers in your church, do you clearly speak against this type of behavior like the Bible says and loose members? It's a pure catch 22 and I may be able to shed some light on this. Let's use another example as we look back to an issue in the 1920's.

In the 1920's, years after lawmakers cracked down on the Klu Klux Klan, and just about disbanded them down to just a few thousand, the Klan felt they needed to get their numbers, power and control back up. So instead of just aiming hatred toward African Americans, they included Catholics, Jews, and even immigrants. The Klan at this time were led by William Joseph Simmons. This was a result of changes in traditional American Society. Most churches had several active members of the Klan in their congregations and did not want to lose those members. At this time, the Klan members in churches now started going to the Christian Ministers who in-turn convinced the rest of their congregations to support the Klan, and also convinced their members that the Klan was not as portrayed by the media and Liberal America.

This was a tactic that paid off and actually got the Klan's numbers up to the millions. They even marched on Washington later that decade. The reason why I brought this up is to show you how tactics are used to sway Christian Ministers to take a position that is clearly against what the Bible teaches (at least according to most interpretations).

So now as we see, due to the emergence of homosexuals flooding churches and filling the collection plates, some preachers are getting on board and coming out in support of this. It's a tactic that's similar in content to the 1920's Klan example. One such example is the Presbyterian Church in Wisconsin ordaining the first openly gay preacher, Rev. Scott Anderson in 2011. This is clearly a tactic that let gays and lesbians know that the church is clearly starting to get behind their movement, and may even be interpreting scripture differently now. This is an invitation if you will for homosexuals to join the faith and to come openly to their place of worship. Some are even performing marriages for same sex couples. Now you also have many of these preachers that won't speak out against such behavior because there are just too many in their congregation, or they just don't want to offend supporters of same sex marriages in their church.

Now there are some that take a strong stance against this and speak on it often, and don't have a problem stating scripture as it is written. One such man who happens to be one of my favorite pastors is Fred Price Jr, the son of Doctor Fred Price Senior. This is a man in which I got some insight and influence for this book.

Fred Price Jr, states that "men laying with men and women laying with women is an abomination to the Lord". He quotes scripture when he speaks on this in the lesson called "The Pursuit of Holiness" he quotes Leviticus 18:23 which states "you shall not lie with a male as with a woman, it is an abomination". Fred Price Jr has stayed true to scripture and to himself and he even speaks about some other unnatural behavior in the same series of lessons such as bestiality and necrophilia. He also states that these things are detestable and sickens the Lord and is a stench to the Lord's nostrils. He goes on to quote many scriptures supporting his teachings including Job 4, Isaiah 34 and the book of Galatians.

While Fred Price Jr continues to teach Bible principles and what is truly in his heart, there are some other preachers whom will remain nameless are accepting unnatural homosexual behavior, and even allow them to marry in their place of worship. Then, there are others who take a more subtle approach and don't speak badly about the behavior, but offer prayers and some support without taking a harsh stance against them, like Joel Osteen.

Joel Osteen seems to take a more subtle approach to this issue, and by no means am I attacking him or Fred Price Jr for that matter for any of their approaches because like I say, it's a catch 22. I'm sure as a Christian, it's difficult to deal with, and I think these two have found the best way for them individually to deal with the issue. But others it seems have deviated from even dealing with this issue, or speaking on it. This may just be a direct result of those in support of same sex marriages, or activities being major contributors in their collection plates.

There were only 5 states where gay and lesbian marriages were legal before 2015 when the first edition of this book was written and they were as follows:

Massachusetts

Connecticut

Iowa-(1st state in the mid-west)

Vermont

New Hampshire-(5th state bill signed by Governor John Lynch)

Now you might say that this was a small number of states and due to other states fighting against same sex marriages that it may not go any further, but if you truly believe that then I'll tell you the one about Santa Claus, the Tooth Fairly, and the Easter Bunny. And if you believe in those, then maybe you may believe that it won't go much further. But remember, it started small with interracial marriages (just a few states) and then it grew into 50 states in a very short period of time.

Are you starting to see the correlation? It is my theory, that in about 5 more years in 2020 same sex marriages will be legal in every state in the Union. Mark my words, in 2020, you will all say Michael, you were right and then we move on to the next fight.

Same sex marriages did become legal in all 50 states by the Supreme Court in 2015. The previous paragraph was from the first addition of this book. It's now 2021 and as you can see, I was correct in my assumption.

This is where we are now, and this is also where we thought we would never be, but here we are knocking on the doorstep of having same sex marriages legal in every state.

Now if your grandparents are still alive or hell, even your parents, put the book down for a second and go ask them how they felt about this issue 30 to 40 years ago. Did you do it? Great! and I can tell you what they said. I betcha, watch this and I quote, "well son or daughter, 30 plus years ago if you would have told me that we would now be on the verge of same sex marriages being legalized, I would have said Strange? Sick? Unbelievable? Twisted? Sounds familiar? Yea, your great grandparents probably said the same thing about 60 plus years ago about interracial marriages.

Gays and lesbians are coming out in larger and larger numbers and in this country, **numbers control politics, politics control politicians, politicians control laws, and laws control people**.

If the previous statement is true, and we know this by history. Then we can rest assure that the numbers are in favor of those in the current fight (same sex marriages).

Thus, same sex marriages did eventually pass in every state because there are millions upon millions of gays and lesbians coming out every day in America and unless this changes, meaning those numbers decline (which they probably won't), we won't be able to do anything to stop this.

Another interesting thing that Fred Price Jr spoke about was that in the days of Noah, before the great flood, 'the normal was abnormal and the abnormal was normal". Just think about that as we will re-visit this in a later chapter.

So where are we going? Well, we now know where we have been and we even know where we are.

Who's on deck?

Who will be the next group to pick up the touch and start the next fight?

Who is in the closet now and lingering in the

woodwork's waiting to take a stand?

Who is paying attention to the same sex rights

movement and now wants their turn?

Well, my guess would be the polygamist.

POLYGAMIST

Before I get into details about this, let me
say that this fight has been probably been
around just as long as interracial marriages,
and same sex marriages. But for some reason,
the numbers have always been pretty small, so
there hasn't been an outpouring of protest or
major attempts to get it legalized. But here is
a theory, and follow me on this.

There has always got to be a reason or excuse
to start a fight or protest. It has to be something
symbolic, and though for some of you reading
this are on the opposite sides of the fence,
including myself on all, but one of these issues,

it is symbolic to those who want these rights. Rights to do what we consider unnatural, and unacceptable behavior.

Before I get into my theory on this, let's take a look at these statistics courtesy of InfidelityFacts. com and I'll explain after we review these stats.

Percentage of marriages that end in divorce in America: 53%

Percentage of "arranged marriages" (where parents pick their sons or daughters spouses) that end in divorce: 3%

Medical field(s) with the highest divorce rate: psychiatrists and marriage counselors

Percentage of marriages where one or both spouses admit to infidelity, either physical or emotional: 41%

Percentage of men who admit to committing infidelity in any relationship they've had: 57%

Percentage of women who admit to committing infidelity in any relationship they've had: 54%

Percentage of men and women who admit to having an affair with a co-worker: 36%

Percentage of men and women who admit to infidelity on business trips: 36%

Percentage of men and women who admit to infidelity (emotional or physical) with a brother-in-law or sister-in-law: 17%

Average length of an affair: 2 years

Percentage of marriages that last after an affair has been admitted to or discovered: 31%

Percentage of men who say they would have an affair if they knew they would never get caught: 74%

Percentage of women who say they would have an affair if they knew they would never get caught: 68%

Now, if look at the bold underline statistic we will see that 41% of those marriages that end in divorce due to infidelity. That's a large number. So where are we going? Well, keep in mind that every fight has a starting point, remember in the introduction where I spoke about how and why the necrophilia fight began, and their reasoning to pass their laws? Well, here is where some polygamist may derive their reasoning for the fight to make polygamy legal. You see, one theory of mine, is that due to infidelity rates being so high at 41 plus %, which clearly affects the divorce rate, polygamist may go on record as saying that, if you let them marry multiple partners, then there would be no reason for divorce. In other words, the divorce rare would go down substantially. Think about it, how many polygamist marriages really do end in divorce? I could not even find a stat on it, but my guess is that it's pretty low because after all; Why would anyone get divorced if they can have their cake and eat it too.

So, we fast forward to 2025ish which is right about the time when the same sex marriage fight comes to an end because right .around 2020ish, it too becomes legal in every state; And here comes the polygamist. Their numbers have multiplied into the hundreds of thousands, and as the march on Washington with their picket signs demanding the opportunity to marry as many people as they so desire, they are saying things in the media like, well if people of different races, religions, and creds can get married, and if people of the same sex can get married, then we should be able to marry as many partners as we would like. They would probably go on to say, "we are not hurting anyone, we just want our rights". Just as the interracial couples, and gays and lesbians have stated before in previous chapters.

Now like I said, this fight has been around for a while but not massive in numbers, but watch as the years progress how those numbers will grow.

Strange huh? Twisted huh? Unbelievable huh? Sick huh? Well, not if you pay attention. Before we get into where we are going with this, let's take a look at how this whole polygamy thing got started.

Polygamy means the state of marriage to many spouses or frequent marriage. Polygamy in the United States probably has been around a long time, but as far as we know it was started by Joseph Smith, the founder of the Latter-Day Saints Movement on July 12, 1843. Other leaders included Brigham Young and Herber Kimball. All three men took several plural wives. Then after Smith's death in 1844, Young felt that the church was secure enough to openly practice polygamy to the rest of the world. It was in 1852. It was about this time that the government threatened to take legal action against the church.

"In 1882, the United States Congress passed the Edmunds Act, which made polygamy a felony". Hundreds of Mormon men and women were arrested. So, the church then decided to ban the practice of polygamy on September 25, 1890.

Thereafter and into today, there are several sects that openly practice or support polygamy. These sects are called The Fundamentalist Church of Jesus Christ of Latter-Day Saints, The Latter-Day Church of Christ, and The Apostolic United Brethren. These groups are currently active in Utah, Arizona, Colorado, and even in Canada. In Utah, there are about 40,000 Mormon Fundamentalist.

Another fact would be, that there are only about 15,000 more people with no church affiliation practicing polygamy.

Now those may be small numbers you might say, and well at this stage you are absolutely right. But keep in mind, we are at least 5 plus years from this fight, and also keep in mind that we are still in the same sex marriage fight. So, these numbers can and will increase.

You see, some will even use the current fight of same sex marriages as a bases to marry multiple partners. And I'm not just taking about men, Yes, I'm speaking about ladies too. Now you might say that men only are interested in marrying multiple partners due to the current state of the Mormon church, but remember, when one starts fighting for their rights, others will follow suit. This is the correlation. This fight might clearly be designed for men wanting multiple partners and wives, but women too will want and desire more partners and husbands as well.

Strange huh? Twisted huh? Sick huh? Unbelievable huh? Well, I think we've been here before in previous chapters and it gets more intense by the minute.

All I can say to you at this point is what would possibly make you think that polygamist will not enter the fight soon, because when you think about it, polygamist; will have some religious basis for their believe, whereas gays, lesbians, and even interracial couple's wont. What I mean by that is that Mormons now use the 1886 revelation to John Taylor as their basis.

John Taylor was the third leader of The Church of Jesus Christ of Latter-Day Saints. The 1886

Revelation was a so-called divine text the he claimed to receive basically stating to re-instate earlier founding principles.

Other religious values, excuses, or reasoning for this would be the Biblical great King Solomon, who had hundreds of wives. Some will definitely use this as a reasoning tool, because he was the wisest king to ever live. Afterall, if the wisest king that ever lived had hundreds of wives, then surely some will say we should follow in his footsteps. This is a common practice of using the Bible and twisting its meaning and substance to your own sick, twisted needs. Slave owners did this with slaves back in the early 1800's. and it wasn't right then, and personally I don't think it's right now. Now I'm sure in about 10 years, if the fight is pretty strong, maybe my mind would even change.

You see, we see these things from afar and use the terms twisted, sick, unnatural, and unacceptable because it's not massive enough to change our minds, and we were all brought up a certain way, but think about it, how many of you have changed your mindset to accept same sex marriages, or even interracial marriages? Well, maybe many of you. So, what makes you think you won't change your mind about polygamy in say about 5 to 10 years, as you see hundreds of thousands protesting and raising awareness on this subject.

The current state of polygamy is primary arranged marriages between younger women, sometimes teenagers and older men. This was a concept that started to raise eyebrows when FBI'S 10 most wanted list Mormon leader, Warren Jeffs took over. Again, let me state it briefly, another way so you can see where I'm going with this, the current state of polygamy entails **younger women being forced to marry older men.** So where will that lead us? Where are we going? when will it stop? Well, think about it for a second? Things progress from bad to worse as the years go by.

So now things get a bit more twisted.

Object sexuality or Ojectophilia.

OBJECT SEXUALITY/OBJECTPHILIA

The year now is about 2027ish, and we as human beings begin to get more and more deplorable and despicable. We have gone from bad to worse in a very short amount of time. We have seen others get their rights in fights that were important to them such as Polygamist and interracial couples and now some others are coming out of the closest.

They are marching and protesting. We've heard it all before. They are using the same phrases like the ones we heard before and I quote, "We aren't hurting anybody, we just want our rights to love as we so choose". They are on the news, and begging the Congress and the Senate to pass a law that will accommodate them.

This Particular group of people are into Objectophlia.

Objectophilia refers to object sexuality. This by definition means a form of sexual or romantic attraction to objects. This can technically be anything solid such as a vehicle, plant, relic, collectible, or any inanimate object. Those who marry or want to marry the object are called Objectophiles.

Now, some of you reading this might find this a bit strange and can't conceive something this bizarre, however; what if I told you that this has been going on for years. Let me give you some examples.

In the year 2009, A lady by the Amy Wolfe fell in love with a fairground ride. Any claims to have had romantic feelings towards the ride and even got jealous whenever someone else was on the ride. The amusement park ride is called 1001 Nacht, which was located in Elyburg, PA at the Knoebels amusement park.

In July of 2009, reports began to surface that Amy even wanted to marry the rollercoaster.

Another example is a guy named Edward who is a TV host in the UK. Edward Smith claims to have had sex with over 1000 cars since he was 15 years old. Edward claims that as a teen, he was tempted to have sex with a Volkswagon Beetle.

Edward stated that "It is hugging and holding the shape of the car close to me and actually talking to it a little bit. And then of course, the rest is just physical satisfaction – masturbation is, I guess, the word.

"It is done with the car, by the car – next to it."

Another example would be a student by the name of Bill Rifka, Bill is actually dating his labtop. Bill says that he and his lab-top are in a homosexual relationship. Bill even states the he has often had urges to get to know other lab-tops but considers that cheating.

The list goes on and on with countless other examples of people just like these. So, where are we going? Remember, as time progress on, we will may see much more of this type of behavior based on previous examples.

Now consider this, maybe a few hundred thousand people are practicing this behavior in 2025ish and the politicians have to make a decision. It's a done deal. Objectophlia is now legal. Remember they have to get votes and the more people concerned about passing a law that they please, they will remain in office.

So now we are on to the next fight. We seen us become somewhat of a civilized society, to becoming more and more open to new sexual experiences. We've seen us come from a place of marriage between a male and female, to accepting several other types of marriages or unions.

Remember, **numbers control politics, politics control politicians, politicians control laws,**

and laws control people. So if the numbers are there, then the laws have to pass.

Now we get into the really twisted and sick. Objects can more than likely lead to our next segment. I would imagine that would be sex and relationships with dolls.

AGALMATOPHILIA

Here we go again people. The marches are on, and the protest are real. Can you imagine it? I can for sure. You see people like I said, one fight leads to the next and in my opinion, we have or will have already gone too far. So, why not take it further. I mean we have already broken norms, and threw most our principles away. Those of us who are not participating in those previous unnatural behaviors listed have learned to accept them as part of our society. We use to frown upon most of them and now we have become immune and numb to the fact that there are some weird things going on around us. I mean just 30 years ago, we frowned upon gays, lesbians, and polygamist: And we probably didn't even know about Objectophilia.

So, we are now getting to the point where we don't even want to have any contact with humans from a relationship standpoint. We are becoming increasingly self- consumed, and our sexual desires have reached the point to where a human being just won't cut it anymore. Imagine getting to the point where your arousal level is beyond what a human can fulfil for you. I'm guessing this is what's happening with those that are ordering sex dolls and they practice Agalmatophia.

Agalmatophilia is defined as a sexual attraction to a statue, doll, or mannequin.

Here we go with the next fight. I quick fact, did you guys know that the original Barbie Doll was based on a sex doll. It's true, in the 1950' Barbie was designed after a German actress for adult males. It was called the Bild Lilli doll.

So, by saying this, by design, this is something that has been being worked on for quite some time.

Another fact is that America is one of the top 5 countries at this point to order sex dolls. It may surprise you that the Philippines are number one: But give it time, I'm sure more and more Americans will move us up into the top by 2030ish. At that point, we will see them coming out in large numbers, maybe in the hundreds of thousands demanding their rights. I mean let's face it, a doll is not going to talk back, ask you to take out the trash, ask you for sex, money, or anything else. It will just be there for your convenience. Now, if you look at it from that stand point, I would imagine, most people would say the heck with human relationships. Think about it, I already showed you how high divorce rates are in this country, so I would guess that these are the reasons why so many are turning to non-humans, and the sex doll gives you a compliant humanoid.

We know how the story ends. Laws are passed to protect those entering into this union to keep the votes and please the constituents. This could very well happen even before the 2030's. Doll fetish is a real thing, and there are dozens of online sites selling them in all different shapes and sizes with working parts for both male and female. Some places even rent them, that's how popular this thing is and it will continue to grow.

This could only cause things to get into the really twisted and sick. Who's up next? Remember one fight leads to another. If you look back at the end of the polygamy section and read the bold statement that states" the current state of polygamy entails **younger women being forced to marry older men.** Well, I'm guessing child/adult unions or marriages.

CHILD MOLESTERS OR ADULTS/CHILD SEX

Well people, the year in 2035ish and the USA is changing for the worse. Things have gotten so out of hand, that we can't seem to get a handle on anything. A few years back we have just legalized polygamy in all 52 states in the union and now the sick and really twisted start to come out. Their numbers were small, at least as far as we know, right around the time I wrote this book. But prisons were filled with them and we even had them register as sex offenders so that everyone could know how sick they were or are. They have been though Chris Hansen's dateline NBC to catch a predator, embarrassed, arrested, and some even put to death. But here they are, as strong as they have ever been, and in large numbers marching on Washington, just like prior groups before them, groups like interracial couples, gays, lesbians, and polygamist.

This is truly a sad day in America as we watch them, and their supporters on the news with their Pickett signs, and bullhorns causing riots and outburst. They are making statements to the news media saying things like, if gays, lesbians, polygamist and interracial couples can marry or have sex, then why can't we have sex with children or minors. They are making other familiar comments like "we are not hurting anyone; we just want our rights". Remember that saying? Well again we hear it, and this time we get sicker to our stomachs, but wait, weren't we sick to our stomachs 10, 20, 30, 40, or even 60 years ago before some of the other things in previous chapters became legal? Remember, yea we were, and then as we got more and more liberal and tolerant to others views and feelings, we toned it down.

So, will we tone this down? Well, my thoughts are that if you are reading this book, it sickens you that I would even suggest such a thing as us toning this one down, but most of us may not even be around then when this comes full circle. Or better yet, it may be sooner then what we think. Remember, each generation, gets more and more liberal and tolerant of unnatural behavior. We did. So why would our kids, kids not be liberal enough to tolerate this type of behavior. I mean, it will be a different time, we are talking in the future some 20 plus years, at least we hope it's far out. I can't tell you exactly when it's coming but I can tell you that its coming.

Let's look back on the last bold statement in the previous chapter, remember what I said about the state of polygamy now? That it usually involves younger women being forced to marry older men. Well, this could very well be the trigger or at least one of the triggers to try and legalize child and adult marriages, and child and adult sexual relationships.

Really strange huh? Really twisted huh? Really unbelievable huh? Really sick huh? I could not agree with you more, yes, it is. So where are we going? How will we get there? Where are we at present with this? Well, I'm going to share with you some things that clearly show we are on our way to this fight and when we get there, it's really gonna start a chain reaction to the truly sick and twisted.

I'm going to go in three segments here, so let's review them before I get into details. Segment 1-The History to present: Segment 2- Present fights on this: And Segment 3-The future fight for this to be legalized. Let's start with the 1st segment.

The issues of child molestation became public in the 1970's and 1980's. Even in the 1920's, with all that was going on then, it was virtually non-existent. National estimates on the trends started in 1948, however; the trend itself can be traced back to 1857 in France where the first recorded reports surface.

Before the 1970's, those who participated in such activities were primarily in secrecy and small in numbers. Now let's look at this, just like groups before in previous chapters we talked about a trend taking place in secrecy and small numbers. Can you see the correlation here? Like interracial marriages, same sex marriages and polygamist, the trend was slow starting and few in numbers. So, in previous years, there was no need to address the issues of child molestation.

In 1968, 44 of the 50 states started to enact laws to combat sexual child abuse and child molestations. Now here's another correlation, if you look at this trend, you'll notice that the 1960's seemed to be a common place for massive numbers of people participating in unnatural behaviors, or at least the un-natural behaviors we spoke about thus far.

We fast forward to 1974, where Congress passed the Child Abuse Prevention and Treatment Act. This was one of the first laws aimed at prosecuting this type of behavior. Also, in 1979, the National Abuse Coalition pushed harder to have Congress to pass many more laws.

In 1986, Congress passed Child Abusive Victims Right Act. This gives children who have been sexually abused civil claims against their accusers. So, we see in the 1980's and 1990's, there were finally laws to prosecute child abusers.

This is a brief history of child sexual abuse, and child sexual abuse laws in the Unites States. So where are we going with this? Well, let's get into segment 2.

So where are we now with this? Well, remember that every unnatural behavior has to have a reasoning behind the fight, or at least a reasoning in the mind of the person or persons who participate in a particular behavior. So, what could possibly be the reason for child/adult marriages? We'll one theory of mine is that teens nowadays are more subject to manipulation from adults. Adults tend to manipulate the minds of children and teens to persuade them to conform to a certain way of life. We then see the children or teens who have been manipulated demanding or asking for what they have conformed too. This is what may probably happen in the future. Instead of adults leading this fight, it may very well be a fight lead by younger boys and girls. Children and teens are becoming more and more susceptible to brain washing every day and I'm not sure we have what it takes to reverse this.

If we look around now, we see over the past 20 years, several cases of adults marrying children. So, we may think this is years out, but actually they've already begun this fight. They are prepping for this future fight already. Adults are marrying children or attempting to marry children in massive numbers in the current era. We are combating this by prosecuting them as much as we can, but their numbers are growing rapidly. There are two segments of this that I want to share with you, and that is teachers, and church leaders. The reason why I picked these two is because they typically have the most influence over our children. The first segment are just a few examples of teachers having sexual relationships with children.

In August of 1998, in California, a teacher was accused of having sex with a 14-year-old babysitter.

In March of 2000, a substitute teacher, in California, was accused of having sex with multiple teenage students.

In November of 2004, in California as well, an ex-principal faces charges of child pornography.

In Delaware, in March of 2007, a teacher was sentenced for an affair with a teenage student.

In South Carolina, January 2005, a teacher was convicted of sex with a minor.

In Kentucky, in May 2007, a teacher admits to having sex with a young boy.

These are just a few examples of how teachers, whom we trust with our children, betraying us in the worst way.

The next set of examples are our spiritual leaders betraying us in the same way:

In Florida, February 1996, a youth minister molested a dozen teenage boys.

In Utah, November 1996, there was the Mormon sex scandals. This is where multiple Mormon leaders were prosecuted for having sex and marrying underage girls.

In Missouri, October 1998, Reverend Gregory Robertson, 40 years of age, was charged with the rape of three teenage girls.

In New Jersey, August of 1999, a Salvation Army minister had to register as a sex offender.

In California, June of 2001, an ex-pastor was suspected of molesting two boys.

In January of 2003, nationwide, rampant sex abuse was found by many priests.

In Virginia, May of 2009, a former church leader pleads guilty to child molestation sex crimes.

These are just a few examples of some of the betrayal that we've encountered, and you can get a feel of how massive the numbers are currently. If we examine this, 30 plus years ago, those numbers were a lot lower. Now in comparison to previous chapters those numbers too were low 30 plus years ago prior to their time. Now if those numbers increased dramatically over the past 30 years, what makes you think that these numbers won't triple or even quadruple over the next 30 plus year. So where are we going with this?

Well, currently, the fight is stalled, but that doesn't mean that those in support of child/adult marriages or child/adult sexual relationships are not fighting for their rights as we speak.

Mary Letuuraneaur, who molested a 12-year-old boy, and then married the boy in 2005 when he was at the legal age of 18.

In the year of 2013, Leah Shipmen, age 42, an ex-teacher married a student that she was accused of molesting when he was 15 years old.

Also in 2013, Kimberly Bynum, age 29, had sex with a 17-year-old minor, but married him to avoid prosecution.

These are examples of those in the current fight, and there are many more not mentioned in this book. Yes, we have guys like Steve Wilkos who stand up against these monsters, but there are just not enough people like him, but we do applaud and support his efforts.

Segment three gets into where will we go with this. Well, if we look at it realistically, only time will tell but as more and more adults molest children, and more and more children marry adults who have molested them, it will become more normal.

So, you may say that the numbers are not there now, right? but you have to admit, those numbers are increasing daily. Remember, 20 years ago, there was no need for Chris Hanson dateline NBC or Steve Wilkos. The reason being is because there wasn't enough reported or recorded cases to start a fight against them. Even law enforcement now has task forces to crack down on this type of behavior but they too are overwhelmed.

Can you hear em people? Can you see them with their picket signs, and bullhorns in 2035ish saying things like "we are not hurting anyone, we just want our rights". I can. I can also hear them saying things like, that young girl or boy wants to marry me and they are old enough to make their own decisions (which clearly, they are not). Now to add to this, I'm sure they would probably say things like "if the interracial couples, gay and lesbian couples, and polygamist can do it, then why can't we"? Trust me people, this will in turn open doors that we never thought possible in this country.

One other important thing to remember about child/adult sexual relationships or marriages, is that a large majority of these relationships come from within the family structure. In other words, **most child molesters are molesting family members.**

Now you may still be in denial, and you may even say, that the buck may stop with polygamy, but again, it was supposed to stop with or interracial marriages and guess what, it didn't.

Even if you are a politician reading this, you may say now, that I would never vote on any law supporting these rights but let's look back on what I said in a previous chapter. **Numbers**

control politics, politics control politicians, politicians control laws, and laws control people. So, in reading this again, if the majority of people support this or are doing this in future years, what makes you think any politician won't support it? Again, most politicians want to keep their jobs. Of course, once they do vote to legalize child/adult marriages, then that's where the rationalizing begins, remember this all too familiar sentence? "We'll; I don't do it, and my kids or family members don't do it, but they are not hurting anyone, and if it will stop child molestation or child abuse, then we should pass the law, it's the right thing to do". On that note, I think you get the point thus far. I think you understand that there is a real and dangerous possibility that some 30 plus, years, adult/child marriages or sexual relationships will become legal.

Strange huh? Twisted huh? Unbelievable huh? Sick huh? Well, I agree, but prepare yourself because its coming. So where are we going? Well, we now know where we were, where we been and where we are headed next and what's to come. So, who's turn is it next? Who's ready to pick up the fight after things get really twisted when child molesters get their rights and laws pasted to protect them? Well, I would have to say those who want to marry their own family members. Incest or incestuous relationships.

INCEST OR INCESTUAL RELATIONSHIPS:

The year is 2040ish, and we are at a place of no return. Child molesters have just scored a major victory some 10 plus years ago. We have become so open in this country that we have very limited control over what goes on here anymore. In front of the white house as well as capitol hill is where they gather. Brother, sister, cousins, aunts, uncles, nieces, nephews, moms and dads. The signs are out, the bull horn is loud, the chants are loud and they are using familiar phrases like "we just want our rights, we are not hurting anyone". Other phases include, if I want to have sex and marry my own child or niece, nephew or cousin, that's my business. They go on future to say you let interracial couples get married, you let gays and lesbians get married, you let polygamist marry multiple wives or husbands, and you even let child molesters marry children, so why can't I marry my own brother, or sister, or mom, or cousin etc.

This is a direct result of the changing times, and now Congress has to make a decision quickly on this. I'm sure it will be easier for them now since they passed the law allowing children to marry or have sexual relationships with adults. So where are we going? Well, let's look at some facts about this.

Incest is a relationship between family members or close relatives. Incest usually

involves a relationship between an adult and child which is a form of child abuse.

Some cultures around the world in ancient times embraced incest such as ancient Egypt, and ancient Greece. Tutankhamun and his half-sister Ankhesermaun were married for example and in ancient Greece Spartan King Leonidas I, married his nice Gorgo. These are just a few examples of incestuous marriages and there were many more.

So as of now we know that those on the picket lines will be using phrases like," we are not hurting anyone, we just want our rights". But in truth just like child/adult marriages they are indeed. You see one of the main problems with an incestuous relationship is that of inbreeding. This causes the children of these so-called relationships to become more susceptible to sickness, diseases and birth disorders. So those of us that are looking to fight against getting legislation passed in reference to this do have some ammo. But is it enough? Well, I would imagine when this time comes, and the numbers are so high of those participating is this type of behavior, or those in support of this will have the numbers on their side and getting back to my theory that" **Number's control politics, politics control politicians, politicians control laws, and laws control people"**, then we know that we may be fighting a losing battle.

One of the things we talked about in previous chapters was that every fight has a trigger, and it is usually from a previous fight. If we look at the previous chapter, the fight for adult/child marriages or sexual relationships, this could very well stem the fight for incest. My theory is that some of those adults who are abusing teens and children are manipulating their minds to control and marry them. They may also be controlling some of their own family members. This is another form of child sexual abuse and in most cases, it usually involves children of the abusers or cousins, nieces and nephews. I found that Father/daughter relationships are among the most common of these. Now in saying that, you can believe that child abusers from within families will step up to this fight.

Sure, there will probably be cousins and uncles, and even sisters and brothers coming forth for the fight, but my theory is that the majority of those fighting this fight, will be adults who have molested their own children or family members, and that they have been left in charge of those children from time to time.

This is a direct result of how far things will go. Some of you reading this may not think it's possible, but if adult/child marriages, and polygamy get legalized, then this is just another step to liberate us and give everyone their rights. Yes, there are some sick and twisted people out here, but all sick and twisted people are sick and twisted in different ways.

You see, some like children, some like multiple marriages at the same time, and some others may like their own family members. It sounds very strange and twisted to me and even to you maybe, but to our ancestors, grandparents, and parents, interracial marriages may have sounded strange and twisted to them, and look at where we are now with that. To some of us same sex marriages sound strange, sick, and twisted, and again, look where we are now with that. This is the true circle of unnatural behavior, it goes on and on to the point where at some point every twisted group would feel that in a free country, they should have those rights. They too feel just like you and I feel about having the right to do some of the things that we do.

There is another aspect of this just like all other fights that proceeded it, and that's the media take on this, the big screen.

Well, there is one such movie that addresses this issue, and that was the movie "Flowers in the Attic". This movie was directed by Jeffrey Bloom starring Louise Fletcher, Victoria Tennant, Kristy Swanson, and Jeb Stuart Adams. This movie came out in 1987 and was remade in 20014. It depicts a brother and sister whose mom locked them in an attic at her father's house, as he was dying so that she can inherent his fortune. The father was not aware that she had children and if he found out, then it would ruin her inheritance. The brother and sister bonded only to realize that they were a product of an insestual relationship. Although the movie was not received too well back in the 1980's. It was however received well in 2014 and from my understanding, they are making a mini-series out of it.

This goes back to what I was saying about the media, and big screen embracing a concept that may not have been popular or accepted at some point (like in the 1980's, a movie about incestuous behavior), then being embraced at some later point in history. So, we see in this example, the movie and book turned heads and was forbidden and highly unacceptable 20 plus years ago. Now it has come to a point of preparing for this as it was re-made in 2014.

So as this fight goes before lawmakers, guess what happens? Well, you guessed right, it passed and now there is a bill on the books to legalize incest and incestuous relationships. It's not hard to imagine, we already crossed the threshold with adult/child relationships.

Really, really strange huh? Really, really twisted huh? Really, really unbelievable huh? Well, at this point, no not really. So' I guess it's time to move on to the next fight. Who's on deck? Who's watch the incestuous fight and waiting their turn, whose numbers are increasing dramatically? Who can't wait to get lawmakers talking about them?

Well, we can only imagine, we have already explored the extreme human sexual perversions, and some of you may even be thinking that it can't get any worse than that.

But can it? Welcome to the extreme twisted section, not that some other chapters were not, but this is beyond your wildest imagination. We'll start with Zoophilia and Bestiality.

ZOOPHILIA AND BESTIALITY:

We'll people, the year is 2045ish and it looks as if we all have lost our way. Things are so out of control that we have in recent years just legalized incest and child/adult marriages. We are so liberal and open to the feelings and rights of others, that we let things that we deem as unnatural as some point in time, become commonplace now. So why would we not legalize zoophilia and bestiality? If we have gone as far as some of the other unnatural behaviors, then why on earth should we deny these sick and twisted individuals their rights?

When they hit Capitol Hill, you better believe that they will be using the same phrases like "we are not hurting anyone, we just want our rights". They would also be saying things like you let gays, lesbians, interracial couples, child molesters, polygamist and those in incestuous relationships get married or have sexual relationships, so why can't we. Do you hear them people? I do. And guess what, ironically, they will have a symbolic point. Because who's to say at this point, where their rights aren't just as important as some of the other unnatural behaviors.

So, what will we do, where are we going with this? Where are we now with this? Where have we been with this? And who is fighting for this currently? Well, let's take a look shall we.

Zoophilia is a sexual fixation with animals. Bestiality is sexual activity between human and animals. The two terms are somewhat interchangeable, one refers to fixation (wanting to see or imagining but maybe not acting on it) but the other refers to the act of doing it.

Reports show the percentage of people who had sexual contact with animals at one point in their lives as 8% for men and 3.6% for women. This is a staggering statistic. That's 8% for men and 3.6% for women. So, with a stat like that, this tells you that this is a serious problem in our society today and needs to be taken seriously. Now imagine if those numbers increase, which history and time tells us it will. Remember in previous chapters, those numbers too were low at some point but as time progressed, major increases took place. Also, if you look at those stats that I just mentioned, I'm sure those numbers were a lot lower 20 plus years ago. Pay attention as those numbers increase over time, just like the others.

Now most of these cases are reported and confined to those living on farms, which would give some explanation on why this is happening, but that doesn't change the fact that it is happening.

Currently there are several forms of Zoophilia and they are as follows:

Human Animal role Players-those who role play with animals.

Romantic Zoophiles-Those who aspire a romantic encounter with animals.

Zoophilic Fatisizers-Those who fantisize about being with animals.

Sadistic Bestials-Those who delight in this behavior due to cults and satanic worship.

Fetishitic Zoophilia-This is one who has a fetish with being with animals or thinks about it often.

Opportunistic Zoophiles-These are people who will jump at any change to have a sexual relationship with animals at any given time.

Exclusive Zoophiles-These are those who are only exclusive sexually with a specific animal or pet.

Studies show that those that are into zoophilia may be caused by a lack of childhood experimentation and abuse. This may cause those individuals to act out and seek sexual relationships with species other than human. These individuals will not seek help for this condition, so it can be difficult to recognize.

Some further research includes that some who practice zoophilia become aroused by only certain animals while others can become aroused by multiple or several species of animals. Research also shows that some of these individuals are not attracted to humans at all.

From a historical and cultural standpoint, there are also instances of this type of behavior shown in the Bible. In Leviticus 18:23 it reads "And you shall not lay with any beast and defile yourself with it, neither shall any women given herself to a beast to lie with it: it is a perversion. Now let's look at this verse for a second, in the same chapter we talked earlier about how this verse also speaks about homosexual activities but over time those who are homosexual, may feel that the scripture can be interpreted different, and may even use the scripture to push their own agenda in a different way, or perhaps it only referred to the Jews at that time, or perhaps it was an Old Testament text which is the old law, and does not apply to modern Christianity as these were not mentioned in the New Testament. We can see clearly from the verse that these were forbidden, yet over time some kind of way, we find a way to counter or justify unnatural behavior (if you consider it unnatural behavior). This is known as selective reasoning where you take one thing and bend it to fit your way of life, or what you feel is right.

So, I put this to you, if this was written in scripture over 4500 plus years ago, then it must have been a common occurrence because the authors of the Bible would not address an issue if it was not an issue. So, if it was an issue that clearly warranted attention from the Bible writers, which I also remind you, that the population of this planet was nowhere near what it is now, then what makes you think that those who practice Zoophilia or secretly participate in these types of activities, are really few and far between. Give it time, and you will see those numbers increase just like other unnatural behaviors do and will over time. Remember all it takes is for another group to come out of the closest and start fighting for their rights and this group is sure to follow.

So, as we progress though this fight, we may see these numbers at somewhere around 22 to 28 percent of Americans by the year 2040ish practicing in some form of zoophilia. It will, just like other unnatural behavior become commonplace.

Now, since the other twisted individuals have come out of the closet, then so will these sick twisted individuals.

So as the fight continues, they are on Capitol Hill with their picket signs and photos of people kissing animals and some even out there with their animal lovers embraced in unity with them, what do you think would happen? Yes, you guessed it, Congress has no choice but to pass some type of legislation giving these individuals their right to marry or have some type of sexual relationship with their pets.

Can you picture it? Can you imagine it? Can you even think about it? Well, weren't you the same person who thought 30 plus years ago, that gays and lesbians would never be able to marry; Or weren't you the same individual who thought 60 plus years ago, that people of different races would never marry? I'm sure you were and just like now, you may still think that 30 plus years from now people wouldn't marry animals, but rest assure when I tell you that it will happen, if we keep going at this rate.

Strange huh? Twisted huh? Sick huh? Unbelievable huh? I think by now you know it's really not. So where are we going? Who is coming out of the closest next? Who will pick up the torch? We'll we go to the most twisted and bizarre, back to where we started, the beginning of this book but yet the end, Necrophilia.

NECROPHILIA

Well people we are finally here, right where we started; But before we get into any detail on this, lets recap shall we:

It all started from Interracial Marriages, then it went to Same Sex Marriages, from there on to Polygamy, soon after Objectophila, then Agalmatophlia, then super twisted with Insest, then Child Molesters or Child Adult Marriages, then it got really twisted and went to Zoophilia and from there we are here (Necrophilia).

We started around the year 2055ish which is where we are finally, we got here from a series of fights, protest, marches and passing laws.

We had to continue to accommodate every right and freedom because we compromised ourselves to accommodate one or two groups. This is where we created our own problem. We let one unnatural behavior get to us, and we felt in our hearts and minds that if we were to help them get their rights, then things would be ok, but it's not. We put our foots in our mouths and we should be ashamed. We perhaps should have fought harder to stop the madness early on but it probably would not have made much difference anyway. Remember my saying **"Number's control politics, politics control politicians, politicians control laws, and laws control people"**, well, this is why we who are sane individuals would have lost. The numbers just aren't there. So, what now? Well, we can talk a little about Necrophilia and give a little history on the subject and see where we are now with this, and then we will possibly come up with some alternatives.

Necrophilia is sexual attraction or sexual contact with the dead or corpses. These individuals are probably the most twisted of them all. Most cases involving necrophilia involves some form of homicide so that the individual can gain sexual satisfaction. Most of those involved in this type of behavior will not achieve sexual satisfaction any other way.

Accounts in history thus far have been far and between but as we have seen over the past few decades, these numbers too have begun to increase. We can also be sure, that there are hundreds if not thousands of people in the U.S.

Practicing necrophilia in secrecy, just as those of other unnatural behaviors have done before they too came out of the closest.

One of the main segments of individuals suffering from necrophilia is serial killers. Some of the world's most prolific serial killers suffered from necrophilia and they include Jeffrey Dahmer, Gary Ridgeway, and British serial killer Dennis Nilsen. Also, keep in mind that the U.S. has the most recorded serial killers in history at any given time.

Now although necrophilia is considered rare due to no real data supporting that there is a significant number of people doing it, it still doesn't change the fact that it's out there, and can and has the potential to grow rapidly over time.

Researchers Rosman and Resnick reviewed 122 cases of necrophilia and concluded the following:

- 68% were motivated by a desire for an unresisting and un-rejecting partner;
- 21% by a want for reunion with a lost partner;
- 15% by sexual attraction to dead people;
- 15% by a desire for comfort or to overcome feelings of isolation; and
- 12% by a desire to remedy low self-esteem by expressing power over a corpse

Their research also shows that those who participate in necrophilia had occupational access to corpses such as morgue attendants, hospital orderly, and cemetery employees. Go figures. Remember in the previous chapter we spoke about research on those who participate in zoophilia primary working on farms, well this is similar. There could be a connection between those who work in a particular field that assumes some type of unnatural behavior. We can even dig deeper into this if we look at those who participate in relationships with children; The majority of those who do based on examples in the chapter on child/adult relationships tend to work with children.

Also, even if we go further, like in the chapter on same-sex marriages, we may even draw a correlation between prisons, where those of the same sex tend to be connected sexually, due to being around those of the same sex for an extended period of time. This could very well be the case in some of our young men and women coming out of prison and changing behavior by being attracted to those of the same sex.

So here we are. From one thing to the next. From being a somewhat civil society, to an embarrassment.

From being people of great or good character and morals, to being people without any of these.

From being the leader of good standards for the rest of the world, to not having any.

From fighting for things that truly matter and shape the face of the planet, to fighting for things that should be criminal in nature.

This is where we are going, give it time. Some of you may not see these things coming but I indeed do and I'm sure if you really take heed to this book or pay attention to what's going on, then you may open your mind.

So obviously, you can see that this fight will show the least resistance in Congress and the White House, and why should it, we allowed ourselves to get to this point. It's very ironic that the worse of the unnatural behaviors is going to pass its laws with the least resistance.

Extremely strange huh? Extremely twisted huh? Extremely sick huh? Extremely unbelievable huh? Well, yes, it is and there is probably not much we can do about it.

So, when is enough-enough I put to you? Where do we draw the line? Should we have stopped at interracial marriages? Or should we stop at same sex marriages? Or maybe even polygamy? That's about the furthest I'm willing to go if at any point it was up to me but it's not, it's up to all of us. Maybe perhaps, some of you think we shouldn't have ever started at all, even with interracial marriages.

Well maybe we can come up with some ideas and shed some light on things in our conclusion.

CONCLUSION

In conclusion, I want to start by a reference made by a famous boxer, most would say he is the greatest of all times, Muhammad Ali. Muhammad Ali did an interview once and spoke about some of the things I talked about in this book, now in the interview he was only referencing interracial marriages but I'm going to use it in a different way.

Let me start by asking a question to each and every one of you. Who are the most intelligent species on the planet? Well, it shouldn't take you long to answer but just in case you didn't know, it is us(humans).

Now let me put a series of questions to you. This series of questions relate to all other species not human.

Series 1

Have you ever seen two male birds' mate? Have you ever seen two female sheep mates? Have you ever seen two male alligators' mate? Have you ever seen two female Wales mate? Have you ever seen two male lions' mate? Have you ever seen two female monkeys' mate?

Series 2

Have you ever seen an adult female cat mate with a male kitten? Have you ever seen an adult male Pig mate with a female piglet? Have you ever seen an adult female dog mate with a male puppy?

Have you ever seen an adult male bear mate with a baby female bear?

Series 3

Have you ever seen a Hippo mate with a tiger? Have you ever seen a giraffe mate with a rabbit? Have you ever seen an elephant mate with a horse? Have you ever seen a shark mate with a croc?

Series 4

Have you ever seen a live snake mate with a dead snake? Have you ever seen a live wildebeest mate with a dead wildebeest? Have you ever seen a live dolphin mate with a dead dolphin?

Series 5

Have you ever seen adult female Polar bear mare with her blood born son? Have you ever seen and adult male zebra mate with his blood born daughter? Have you ever seen a female kangaroo mate with her blood born brother? Have you ever seen a male monkey mate with his female sister?

Series 6

Have you ever seen a tiger mate with a tree?

Have you ever seen a monkey mate with a doll?

I'm guessing your answer is no to most if not all of these questions, and the reason being is because they meaning animals consider this unnatural in nature. So, if we look at this realistically, how can we as humans (the so called most intelligent species on the planet) not consider some of these things to be unnatural as well. If we send men to the moon, walk upright, build skyscrapers, build airplanes, discover gravity, break the sound barrier, send rovers to mars, discover cures for diseases, do open heart surgeries, and write books, then why is it so difficult for use to not participate in behaviors that are deemed unacceptable to animals? Animals who we have as pets and are subjective and somewhat slaves to us. If it's all unnatural behavior to them, then it should very well be unnatural behavior to us. After all, we rule the planet and set the trends.

So now let's look at the Biblical perspective of these things. I'm not here to preach to you, we will only take a look at the book of Leviticus 18:22-23. Verse 22 reads "Thou shall not lie with mankind, as with womenkind: it is an abomination." Now the word abomination is one the bible uses frequently to describe activity beyond sin. We all know what sin is, but if something is an abomination to the almighty, then that means it really sickens him, meaning it is worse than sin itself. Fred Price Jr. Describes abominations as activities that came to the planet after the fall of lucifer (satan) and the rest of the angels who were kicked out of heaven. He goes on further to say that an abomination leaves a foul order or stench in the nostrils of the almighty. So why on each would anyone want to make the almighty really look down on them by participating in certain types of behaviors. Let me re-iterate, I'm not attacking anyone, I'm simply making points here, you are all human beings and you have your own beliefs and that's your own free will. I will always respect that.

Verse 23 reads "Neither shall thou lie with any beast to defile thyself therewith: neither shall any women stand before a beast to lie down thereto: it is confusion. This is yet just another verse speaking of unnatural behavior. It's a direct reference to zoophilia. Again, even the almighty is against unnatural behavior.

One interesting thing about this is that even back in Biblical times all these unnatural behaviors existed. This should tell you that these behaviors are not new. Even more shocking is that unnatural behavior perhaps may have been the reason for the great flood of Noah (if it happened), to cleanse the earth. Think about it, as bad as things are going now around the world, it's still not bad enough for God or the source to wipe away or cleanse the planet. This should tell you that it was much worse then. In other words, all these unnatural behaviors would have been quite common at that time.

We can even quote Fred Price Jr again by saying "that the abnormal was the normal". So, when abnormal behavior becomes normal, then we condition our minds to accept it and that abnormal behavior now becomes acceptable. A perfect example of this would be black on black crime in most of the larger urban communities across America. Some 40 plus years ago this would have been unacceptable behavior as well, and there is no way anyone could have predicted that it would get this bad, but it has, and we have somehow conditioned ourselves to accepting it, and we are not really doing much as a country to stop it.

Some of these unnatural behaviors may and should possibly be accepted but the problem is if we accept one, at some point, we may have to accept another and another, because more and more people will come out in support of it as time progresses. Remember my saying **"Number's control politics, politics control politicians, politicians control laws, and laws control people".** So, if the numbers are there, then we can't win the fight. The only way to fight some of these unnatural behaviors is to educate others as well as ourselves to perhaps keep our children from making harsh sexual decisions that will cause more harm than good, and also keep some of these behaviors out of the mainstream media, at least for kids to see because they pick up on things and run with what's in most of the time.

So where are we going? Who's up next? Who's waiting? Well, perhaps sexual relationships with spirits, ghost, robots, aliens, entities or other dimensional beings? Think it won't or hasn't happened? Stay tuned for Unnatural Behavior 2.

REFERENCES

Source: Head, Tom, "Interracial marriage laws-A short Time-line history". Aboutnews.com

Source: Head, Tom, "Interracial marriage laws-A short Time-line history". Aboutnews.com

Source: Rose, William "Guess Who's Coming to Dinner', 1967 Film,

Source: Roddenberry, Gene, "Star Trek", The series, 1968

Source: Bower, Lisa. Life123. "The History of Same Sex Marriages"

"Same-Sex Marriages" Wikipedia, The Free Encyclopedia, Wikipedia Foundation Inc. (09/02/2015), Assessed (09/15/2015) <url>

Source: Neil Jordan, "The Crying Game", 1992 Film

Source: Ang Lee, "Brokeback Mountain", 2006 Film

Source: Max Mutchnick, David Koran, "Will & Grace"-TV Series

Christopher Lloyd, Steven Levitan, "Modern Family", TV Series

Barbara Hall, "Madam Secretary", TV Series

Bruno Heller, "Gotham", TV Series

Lee Danials, Danny Strong, "Empire", TV Series

"Same-Sex Marriages" Wikipedia, The Free Encyclopedia, Wikipedia Foundation Inc. (09/02/2015), Assessed (09/15/2015) <url>

Source: Price, Fred Jr., FJ320A, "The Pursuit of Holiness-Lesson"

Source: Orsteen, Joel, "Peirs Morgan Tonight", TV show

Source: Price, Fred Jr., FJ227B, "The Pursuit of Holiness"-Lesson

"Polygamy" Wikipedia, The Free Encyclopedia, Wikipedia Foundation Inc. (14/02/2015), Assessed (16/02/2015) <url>

King James Version, "The Holy Bible"

"Child Sexual Abuse" Wikipedia, The Free Encyclopedia, Wikipedia Foundation Inc. (14/02/2015), Assessed (5/02/2015) <url>

Source: Sheperdson, Donald, "Creating Safer Havens", 1998-2015

Source: Sheperdson, Donald, "Creating Safer Havens", 1998-2015

Source: "The Huffington Post" 1/23/2013

Wilkos, Steve, "The Steve Wilkos Show" TV Show

Source: Hanson, Chris, "To Catch a Predator", TV Show

"Incest" Wikipedia, The Free Encyclopedia, Wikipedia Foundation Inc. (26/02/2015), Assessed (25/02/2015) <url>

"Zoophilia" Wikipedia, The Free Encyclopedia, Wikipedia Foundation Inc. (24/02/2015), Assessed (04/03/2015) <url>

"Necrophilia" Wikipedia, The Free Encyclopedia, Wikipedia Foundation Inc. (02/04/2015), Assessed (04/03/2015) <url>

Source: (2/27/2012). Divorce and the lds church. (online)m 12/30/2015 http://www.religioustolerence.org/lds divo.htm

Source: (2020). 10 People who fell in love with inanimate objects. (online), 2/15/2022 10 People who fell in Love with Inanimate Objects | Futurescopes.

www.ingramcontent.com/pod-product-compliance
Lightning Source LLC
Chambersburg PA
CBHW051458250726
48655CB00001B/477